Original title:
The Frost Path

Copyright © 2024 Swan Charm
All rights reserved.

Author: Mirell Mesipuu
ISBN HARDBACK: 978-9908-52-098-8
ISBN PAPERBACK: 978-9908-52-099-5
ISBN EBOOK: 978-9908-52-100-8

Frost Enshrouded Echoing Souls

In the stillness of the night,
Whispers dance in pale moonlight.
Starlit shadows gently glide,
Frost enshrouded, hearts decide.

Voices carried on the breeze,
Echoes woven through the trees.
Silent secrets softly shared,
In the cold, the beating dared.

Memories like snowflakes drift,
In the dark, our spirits lift.
Frozen tears and laughter bright,
Soulful echoes in the night.

Stardust glimmers, hopes entwined,
In this realm, our fates aligned.
Weaving threads of dreams anew,
Frost enshrouded, spirit's view.

Amidst the chill, we find a spark,
Illuminating paths so dark.
As the dawn begins to break,
Echoing souls, we gently wake.

Crystal Echoes of a Shivering Dawn

Morning light begins to creep,
Awakening the world from sleep.
Crystal echoes ring so clear,
In the chill, we feel no fear.

Gentle mist wraps round the trees,
Whispers float upon the breeze.
Sunrise paints the sky so bright,
Chasing off the cloak of night.

Frozen droplets shining bright,
Glistening with the morning's light.
A shivering dawn breaks the gloom,
Life erupts, the flowers bloom.

Softly calling, nature sings,
A symphony of new beginnings.
In this moment, hearts take flight,
Crystal echoes, pure delight.

Together in this fleeting time,
Our spirits dance, an endless rhyme.
As the dawn begins to rise,
We embrace the morning skies.

Echoes of a Frozen Symphony

In the silence, whispers play,
Notes suspended, drift away.
Chilled breezes hum their tune,
Underneath the icy moon.

Strings of frost in twilight's glow,
Dance upon the winter's snow.
Melodies of past entwine,
Crafting dreams in frozen time.

Frost-laden Dreams Unraveled

Beneath the stars, a vision waits,
Dreams adorned with icy gates.
Faded echoes softly sigh,
In the stillness, shadows lie.

Crystals gleam like whispered hopes,
Floating high on winter slopes.
Every breath, a frosty kiss,
A fragile moment filled with bliss.

Seasons of Ice and Wonder

Time stands still in silver light,
Frozen fields, a wondrous sight.
Nature's art in every flake,
Beauty born in winter's wake.

Glistening branches touch the sky,
Whispers echo, soft and shy.
World adorned in purest grace,
Embracing solitude's embrace.

A Tapestry of Crystalline Whispers

Threads of ice weave tales untold,
In shimmering patterns, bold.
Every flurry speaks in hues,
Of frosty dreams and morning dew.

Luminous shards in twilight's hand,
Crafting stories, a magic strand.
In the quiet, secrets twine,
As winter's breath weaves every line.

Shivering Leaves in Hibernation

Leaves quiver in the cold,
Their stories left untold.
Whispers through the barren trees,
Nature sighs a whispered breeze.

Branches bare, a somber sight,
Holding on to fading light.
The earth prepares for dreams to sleep,
While shadows in the silence creep.

In twilight's golden glow,
A dance of flakes, soft and slow.
The ground, a quilt of winter's thread,
Cradles all, softly spread.

Beneath the frost, a secret waits,
Life's pulse in hibernation states.
Silent whispers in the dark,
Awaiting spring's resurgent spark.

Time slows in this frozen pause,
Nature rests without a cause.
Shivering leaves in quiet nights,
Dream of warmth, of future sights.

The Stillness of Frosted Night

Moonlight drapes the world in white,
Stars like diamonds, pure and bright.
Silent streets, no sound, no cheer,
All is calm; the night is here.

A crystal blanket hugs the ground,
In this peace, no heartbeat found.
Breath hangs heavy in the air,
Frozen dreams in silence share.

Each shadow cast, a story told,
Beneath the frost, the night is bold.
Knots of ice on window panes,
Nature's art, where beauty reigns.

Look beyond the stillness deep,
Where secrets in the starlight creep.
A world asleep, yet oh so bright,
The magic of this frosted night.

Time stands still, and hearts beat slow,
In the moon's soft and silver glow.
Moments weave a tranquil lace,
In the stillness, find your place.

Guardians of the Icebound Realm

Silent sentinels stand tall,
Guardians of the frost-bound hall.
With arms outstretched to icy skies,
Ancient whispers, nature's ties.

Evergreens embrace the chill,
Their fragrant breath, a winter thrill.
Beneath the drifts, their roots grow deep,
While watchful shadows weave and creep.

Creatures stir beneath the snow,
Seeking warmth, where soft winds blow.
In this realm, a solemn vow,
To shield the earth, here and now.

Icicles hang like crystal swords,
Nature's defense, with no rewards.
Each flake a promise, pure and true,
Guardians all, both old and new.

Here they stand through night and day,
In silence, keeping dark at bay.
Embracing winter's icy breath,
Guardians of life, even in death.

Echoes in the Glinting Snow

Footsteps crunch on winter's glow,
Echoes dance in glinting snow.
Every step a story shared,
In this world, all hearts laid bare.

Whispers float on the frosty air,
Moments linger, memories rare.
The glimmering white, a canvas pure,
In its embrace, we feel secure.

Trees stand watch, like ancient kings,
Holding secrets of life's springs.
Each flake catches the fleeting light,
Echoes fade into the night.

In waltz of snowflakes, dreams arise,
Beneath the cold, a warm surprise.
Echoes wrapped in winter's arms,
A symphony of softest charms.

As shadows stretch and daylight wanes,
The world outside subtly gains.
Echoes in the glinting snow,
Forever linger, ever flow.

Beneath the Quiet of Silent Snows

Beneath the quiet of white snows,
Whispers of winter gently flows.
Soft blankets cover the sleeping ground,
In this stillness, peace is found.

Branches heavy, draped in white,
Stars twinkle softly, a guiding light.
Footsteps muffled in the cool, crisp air,
Nature's canvas, pure and rare.

Frozen lakes mirror the vast sky,
As winds of change begin to sigh.
A world transformed, serene and bright,
Wrapped in the calm of winter's night.

Frozen Footprints of the Past

Frozen footprints mark the way,
Echoes of footsteps from yesterday.
Stories linger in every stride,
As time slips gently, a fleeting tide.

Paths once bright with laughter and cheer,
Now silent whispers, memories near.
Each step in snow, a tale unfolds,
Of winter's chill and dreams untold.

In the quiet, reflections call,
Frozen moments, we once stood tall.
While shadows lengthen with the day,
The past remains, never to stray.

Mirrored Silence in Moonlit Frost

In mirrored silence, the moonlight gleams,
Frosty patterns weave through dreams.
A hush blankets the world so wide,
As night enfolds, and stars reside.

Each crystal flake, a fleeting wish,
Dancing softly, like a lover's kiss.
The earth adorned in silver lace,
Under the watchful moon's embrace.

Stillness reigns in the midnight hour,
A moment's pause, a timeless power.
In this beauty, hearts take flight,
Beneath the glow of the frosty light.

Chasing Shadows on Icy Paths

Chasing shadows on icy paths,
Softly gliding, the spirit laughs.
Footprints etch tales in the frost,
In this dance, all worries are lost.

Moonbeams guide in the cold night air,
Whispers of winter wrapped in care.
Every slide, each twirl and spin,
Bringing joy from deep within.

Around the corners, laughter rings,
As fleeting moments share their wings.
Chasing shadows, we find our way,
In the beauty of a winter's play.

Fragments of a Hushed Winter

Snowflakes dance in silence,
Whispers of the cold night,
Branches wear their crystal coats,
Nature's breath held tight.

The moon spills silver shadows,
Over fields dressed in white,
Echoes of forgotten warmth,
In this frozen light.

Every sound feels hushed now,
Steps muffled in the frost,
Time has wrapped its arms tight,
In this stillness, we're lost.

A world caught in a moment,
Where dreams and silence blend,
Each breath is a fragile secret,
Winter's lullaby, our friend.

Fragments of a gentle memory,
Drifting on the wind's sigh,
In this hush, we find solace,
As fleeting moments fly.

Still Spirits Beneath the Snow

Beneath the quilt of winter,
Life dreams beneath the chill,
Whispers of untouched beauty,
Awaiting spring's first thrill.

A ghostly air surrounds me,
Footsteps lost to the past,
Nature's breathless waiting,
For the warmth to come at last.

Pine trees stand as sentinels,
Guardians of frozen nights,
Their secrets buried deeply,
In the soft, silvery heights.

Shadows play in twilight,
As the sun begins to fade,
Echoes of the living,
In this stillness, they are laid.

The spirits of the season,
Resting 'neath the cold white,
Yet promise of rebirth lingers,
In the heart of winter's night.

The Isolation of Frozen Landscapes

In the distance, mountains linger,
Veiled in a breath of snow,
Whispers of frost-bitten silence,
Where only the cold winds go.

Trees stand stiff and lonely,
Their silhouettes stark and bare,
Caught in the web of winter,
In this vast, empty air.

Frozen lakes mirror the sky,
A canvas of pale despair,
Yet beneath the ice, there's life,
In each still moment, they share.

Isolation wraps around me,
Like a shroud of icy breath,
Yet in this desolate beauty,
I find a quiet depth.

The landscapes speak in silence,
In tones gentle, yet low,
A reminder that in stillness,
We can learn to let go.

Wandering Through Frosted Memories

Each step is a careful echo,
On paths of glimmer and frost,
Memories swirl like snowflakes,
In the moments we thought lost.

The air is crisp with whispers,
Of laughter from days gone by,
Yet the chill holds their reflections,
In the heart of the winter sky.

Trees, bare and bending slightly,
Mark the trails I used to roam,
In this landscape of silence,
I still feel a flicker of home.

Ghosts of a playful spirit,
Linger in the playful snow,
In the fold of every shadow,
Lie stories we used to know.

Wandering through frosted memories,
Time stretches like the night,
Carried by winter's stillness,
To where the past feels right.

Mirror of the Winter Sun

In the stillness of dawn, the frost gleams bright,
A polished surface where dreams take flight,
The sun half-hidden behind the icy veil,
Whispers of warmth in the chill prevail.

Reflections dance in the silver light,
Every glimmer a secret, pure delight,
Branches weave stories in soft-spoken hues,
Nature's canvas dressed in frosty blues.

The world holds its breath beneath blankets white,
Waiting for color to break the night,
With every ray, destiny is spun,
As the heart beats softly, a waking sun.

Silent Songs of the Frozen Grove

In the hush of snow, the trees stand tall,
Silent songs of winter in a crystal thrall,
Branches bow low, cradling the cold,
Tales of the past in whispers retold.

Each flake that falls, a note on the breeze,
Harmonies echo through frozen trees,
Voices of winter, soft as a sigh,
Under the blanket of the thawing sky.

With every rustle, a secret concealed,
In the heart of the grove, magic revealed,
Footsteps of silence, the choir of night,
Melodies linger in silver light.

Touch of the Ice King

The Ice King sits on a throne of frost,
In a realm where warmth is eternally lost,
His breath a whisper, a chilling caress,
In the court of winter, he reigns to bless.

Icicles shimmer like jewels on high,
Crafted from dreams of a darkened sky,
He dances with shadows, a ghostly glide,
In the still of the night, where secrets reside.

A touch so cold yet oddly divine,
Every crystal droplet a memory's sign,
He holds the world in his icy embrace,
A fleeting moment, a stunning grace.

The Lure of Crystalline Paths

Through the woodlands, whispers beckon near,
Crystalline paths that shimmer and clear,
Inviting wanderers to tread their way,
In the heart of winter, where shadows play.

Footfalls echo on a blanket of white,
Each step a journey, each turn a delight,
The magic of frost paints a story anew,
Illuminated gently by skies of blue.

Nature's invitation, soft as a sigh,
Draws the soul to traverse and fly,
With every glimmer, a promise to find,
The beauty of winter, a gift, unconfined.

Frosted Footsteps of Dawn

In the quiet morn, dew does gleam,
Footsteps whisper, as if in a dream.
Nature awakens, the world feels new,
Warmth of the sun, in a sky of blue.

Birds begin singing, a gentle song,
In frost-kissed fields, where we belong.
Shadows retreat, day takes its stance,
In the golden glow, we find our dance.

Each blade of grass, a diamond bright,
Reflecting the hope of pure delight.
Together we'll wander this peaceful space,
In the frosted footsteps, we find our grace.

The chill lingers on, but hearts grow warm,
In nature's embrace, we weather the storm.
With laughter and joy, we'll carry the load,
As dawn breaks softly, along our road.

Lurking Beneath the Ice

Underneath the frost, secrets reside,
Whispers of winter, a chilling guide.
In waters so deep, shadows intertwine,
A world held still in a crystalline shrine.

Each crack of the surface, a tale to unfold,
Of creatures and dreams, both timid and bold.
Beneath porcelain layers, life waits and hides,
In silence it stirs, where time divides.

What stories are kept in the depths below?
What wonders await in the moon's soft glow?
As lanterns of ice shimmer and sway,
We peer into darkness, enchanted to stay.

Come wander with me, through this frozen realm,
Where nature's magic takes the helm.
In every still moment, there's life to behold,
A tapestry woven in silver and gold.

A Journey Through Winter's Veil

Veils of white blanket the sleeping earth,
In tranquil stillness, we find our mirth.
Each footstep forward in snow so bright,
Guides us through day, and into the night.

Frosted branches, a delicate sight,
Whisper their secrets, silent and light.
With every brisk breath, the world slows down,
In the crisp, pure air, we wear winter's crown.

Time dances lightly on layers of frost,
In the beauty of winter, we feel no cost.
Nature's embrace, a cold but kind friend,
Together we wander, hand in hand 'till the end.

The moon softly glimmers on pathways unknown,
With beauty unyielding, our hearts have grown.
We'll carve out our stories, amidst the chill,
In winter's soft tapestry, we find our will.

Shards of Crystal Light

In morning's embrace, the world aglow,
Shards of crystal light dance to and fro.
A prism of colors, where shadows play,
Glistening beauty in the heart of the day.

Through forests adorned, a shimmering trail,
Each step resonates, telling a tale.
The snowflakes twinkle, like stars in the night,
Covering the earth in pure delight.

With each gentle gust, the crystals rise,
The world transforms beneath morning skies.
Nature's artistry, wild and unconfined,
In the radiance woven, our souls entwined.

Amidst the brilliance, our spirits take flight,
In this fleeting moment, hearts feel the light.
Together we stand, in the glow that remains,
In shards of crystal, love forever gains.

Glacial Choir in Stillness

In quiet depths, the silence sways,
The glacial voices softly play,
Whispers weave through icy peace,
A timeless song that will not cease.

Drifting snowflakes weave and twirl,
Nature sings in crisp unfurl,
Harmonies in chilling air,
Each note a breath, a frozen care.

Amidst the blue, the world stands still,
Echoes of frost fulfill the chill,
Every flake a story told,
In winter's grasp, the warmth enfold.

Icicles glisten in pale light,
A glacial choir takes to flight,
Underneath the starry dome,
Serenity calls this place home.

The world is hushed, the tones refine,
In every beat, the spirits align,
A symphony of ice and snow,
In stillness, life begins to flow.

Chilled Echoes of Solitude

In the quiet of the night,
Chilled echoes take their flight,
Whispers float on frosty breeze,
Filling spaces with unease.

Lone shadows dance on snow's embrace,
Memories linger, time's trace,
Each step crunches, breaking peace,
Winter's grip will never cease.

A distant howl, the moonlight fades,
Solitude in frozen shades,
Every flake a thought of loss,
Each heartbeat aches, a heavy cost.

Stars above like diamonds gleam,
Frigid dreams merge with the stream,
In this realm, the chill won't part,
Echoes linger in the heart.

Through silent woods, the night extends,
In every turn, solitude bends,
Chilled echoes whisper lowly here,
In icy grasp, they draw me near.

Twilight on a Frozen Stream

Twilight paints the icy flow,
Amber hues on sheets of snow,
Glistening like forgotten dreams,
In the hush, the stillness seems.

The river rests beneath the freeze,
Time's gentle hand, a soft tease,
Reflections flicker, dance, and play,
As colors merge, then fade away.

Silent realms where shadows creep,
Nature holds her secrets deep,
Beneath the ice, a world persists,
In twilight's glow, it gently twists.

Beneath the sky's violet embrace,
The water's pulse leaves not a trace,
Stillness reigns where ripples should,
In frozen dreams, the silence stood.

The day retreats, night takes its place,
On the stream, a tranquil grace,
Twilight whispers, sweet and clear,
In frozen beauty, winter's cheer.

Memories Carved in Ice

Carved in ice, the moments freeze,
Whispers caught in winter's breeze,
Every shape a tale retold,
In crystal dreams, the past unfolds.

Faces of friends, laughter bright,
Captured in the silver light,
Fleeting joys of yesteryears,
Echoes soft, like distant cheers.

As frosty winds begin to blow,
Each memory, a gentle glow,
Guardian of all that was,
Frozen time, a sacred cause.

Yet in the chill, there lies a spark,
A warmth within the winter's dark,
Though ice may bind, the heart stays free,
Each memory, a part of me.

As seasons change, and rivers flow,
In silent nights, the memories grow,
Carved in ice, they shine so bright,
Forever held in winter's light.

Shadows of a Sleepy Frost

In twilight's hush, the shadows creep,
Beneath the frost, the world's asleep.
A gentle glow in silver trails,
Whispers of winter, soft as gales.

Branches arch with icy grace,
Silhouettes in a frozen embrace.
The moonlight glints on quiet streams,
Awakening the night's soft dreams.

Each breath releases ghostly sighs,
As stars adorn the velvet skies.
Nature rests in silent charms,
Wrapped warmly, in winter's arms.

Footsteps muffled, hear them tread,
Over the whispers of the dead.
A world transformed, with frosty sheen,
In shadows deep, and soft serene.

Frosty Veils of Forgotten Whispers

Beneath the frost, old stories lie,
Veiled in whispers, soft and shy.
Echoes dance on icy breath,
Memories woven in the threads of death.

A forgotten song on a winter's night,
Calling forth the lost delight.
Snowflakes swirl in delicate twirls,
Painting the air with winter's pearls.

In the stillness, secrets bloom,
Lifting shadows from the gloom.
The frost is a cloak, a soft disguise,
Hiding dreams, where silence flies.

With gentle hands, the dawn will trace,
Each frozen thought, each hidden place.
In the warmth of light, they'll rise again,
To tell their tales, to be seen, my friend.

Dance of the Crystal Light

In crystal light, the world does sway,
A shimmering dance and bright display.
Reflections swirl on silver lakes,
As nature laughs, and the whole earth quakes.

Frosted branches reach and bend,
Glimmers of magic that never end.
The sun awakes with a golden brush,
Painting the morn in a gentle hush.

Each flake a dancer, each gust a song,
Together they waltz, where dreams belong.
Underneath the cerulean skies,
Hope and joy in the frosty ties.

The warmth of life amidst the chill,
In every moment, timeless thrill.
Crystal light, a soft embrace,
Life's dance unfolds in frozen space.

Haunting Paths through the Winter's Grip

Through winding paths where shadows blend,
The winter's grip has tales to send.
Silent whispers of the night,
Guide the wanderer, lost in flight.

Frosty crystals on the ground,
Muffled echoes, a mournful sound.
Every step on icy lace,
Leaves a trace in this haunted place.

Beneath the branches, dark and deep,
Lies the promise of secrets to keep.
In the silence, fears reside,
Yet beauty blooms on winter's tide.

The heart beats slow with every sigh,
In this realm where shadows lie.
Yet even in frost, warmth may start,
A flicker ignites within the heart.

Glacial Hues at Dusk

The sun descends in muted glow,
A canvas rich with icy flow.
The sky, a blend of blue and gray,
Whispers promise of the day.

Silent echoes fill the air,
Frozen branches, stark and bare.
Shimmering hues on snowflakes dance,
In twilight's grasp, a fleeting chance.

Shadows stretch as day takes flight,
Pink and amber, fading light.
A chill that tugs at every breath,
In nature's grip, a taste of death.

With each moment, colors blend,
A quiet beauty that won't end.
Glacial hues, a tranquil sight,
Holding secrets of the night.

Depths of the Frosted Woodlands

In the depths of winter's heap,
Woodlands rest in icy sleep.
Snow-covered trails wind and weave,
Whispers of the night, believe.

Knotted branches, trunks of gray,
Nature's art in disarray.
Frosted ferns and icy breath,
A peace found in the stillness left.

The crunch of snow beneath my feet,
A rhythm slow, a heart's retreat.
Cherished hues of winter's song,
In these woods, I know I belong.

Shadows move, and creatures hide,
Softly dreaming, side by side.
Each corner holds a haunting grace,
In frosted woodlands, time slows its pace.

The Beauty of Winter's Embrace

Winter's breath, a soft caress,
Wrapped in warmth, a pure finesse.
A landscape dressed in glimmering white,
Holding secrets of the night.

Distant mountains, sharp and clear,
Calling forth a world sincere.
Frosted pines in silent prayer,
Echoes of a time laid bare.

Each flake falling, a gift from above,
Nature's way of showing love.
Beauty lies in every breath,
Winter's charm defying death.

In the hush, the world reflects,
Moments lost in winter's depths.
A tapestry of calm and grace,
In winter's arms, a warm embrace.

Frosted Leaves and Shattered Dreams

Frosted leaves cling to the ground,
In the silence, echoes found.
Whispers of a warmth long gone,
Shattered dreams of dawn's sweet song.

Each breath a cloud in winter's chill,
Heartbeats mimic nature's will.
Colors fade, and time stands still,
The earth wrapped in a shivering thrill.

Memories dance with shadows cast,
A reminder of the past.
Leaves of fire now crisp and brown,
Winter's hold, a solemn crown.

Yet beauty lies in every sigh,
Though dreams may fade, they seldom die.
In frosted leaves, we find our way,
Through shattered dreams, we'll still stay.

Frozen Dreams in Twilight

In the quiet dusk, shadows play,
Whispers of night in a soft ballet.
Stars shimmer with a gentle glow,
Dreams drift softly, as cold winds blow.

Crystal edges on the frozen streams,
Wrap the world in silvered dreams.
A hush descends, the air grows thin,
Awakening echoes of where we've been.

The moonlight dances on the trees,
Carrying tales upon the breeze.
Each branch a story, each leaf a sigh,
As memories linger, then softly die.

Under the stars, a blanket of frost,
Memory's warmth, yet never lost.
Frozen dreams in the cool twilight,
Cradled softly in the arms of night.

Awaits the dawn, with its warm embrace,
To melt away this gentle space.
But for now, in this hushed gleam,
We linger still in frozen dream.

The Chill of Solitude

Beneath the weight of silent skies,
Loneliness whispers, softly sighs.
In shadows cast by fading light,
Frosted silence fills the night.

The cold wraps tight, a whispered call,
Echoes of life, where shadows fall.
Each breath a cloud against the air,
Drifting dreams of a world so rare.

In the heart of winter's freeze,
Solitude wears a cloak of ease.
Yet in its chill, a longing grows,
A craving for warmth that nobody knows.

The stars are distant, cold and bright,
Observing my dance in the fading light.
Each twinkle a reminder of places near,
Frozen in time, yet beckoning here.

In stillness deep, I find my peace,
As moments stretch and worries cease.
The chill of solitude, a quiet grace,
In this frozen world, I find my place.

Veils of Sparkling Mist

Morning breaks with a gentle caress,
Veils of mist in their soft dress.
Sparkling diamonds in the light,
Nature's whisper, pure delight.

The earth adorned in crystal lace,
Every corner, a hidden space.
Within the fog, adventures wait,
Mysteries twine, it's never late.

As footsteps echo on gravel ground,
A symphony in silence found.
The beauty lies in what's concealed,
The heart of nature, softly revealed.

Birdsong breaks the morning still,
Awakening life, a gentle thrill.
Through veils of mist, the day unfolds,
A story of wonder, forever told.

In sparkling moments, we find our aim,
Nature painted without a frame.
Lost in the beauty that softly lifts,
We dance along with the sparkling mists.

Trails on a Silver Canvas

Underneath the wide, starry sky,
Footprints linger where dreams lie.
Each step a story, each trail a song,
Dancing echoes of where we belong.

The moon reflects on the tranquil sea,
Silver canvas of what's to be.
With whispers of night and the tide's embrace,
We move as one in time and space.

Waves caress the shore with grace,
Unraveling dreams in this sacred place.
Every ripple, a heartbeat's call,
Guiding us through the night's enthrall.

Ink of shadows written in the sand,
Marks of memories, the heart's command.
As the horizon blushes with dawn,
The trails we leave will carry on.

Beneath the starlight, paths unite,
We walk together into the light.
On a silver canvas, our stories blend,
In the vastness of night, we find our end.

Luminescence in the Quiet Snow

In the stillness of the night,
Snowflakes swirl, a soft delight.
Glowing softly, pure and bright,
Whispers dance in pale moonlight.

Silent fields, a blanket white,
Footprints vanish out of sight.
Trees adorned in frosted light,
Nature smiles, serene, polite.

Frozen rivers gently flow,
Beneath the skin of coldest snow.
Reflecting dreams in gentle glow,
Eternal peace, a sweet tableau.

Stars above begin to shine,
In this world, all feels divine.
Moments linger, hearts entwine,
In the snow, your hand in mine.

Life pauses, just for a while,
As we walk, we share a smile.
In this calm, we find our style,
Joy is here, in winter's aisle.

Secrets in the Icy Gloom

Whispers linger in the air,
Icy fingers wrap with care.
Secrets hidden, unaware,
In the dark, a silent prayer.

Trees stand stoic, cloaked in frost,
Memories of warmth, they lost.
In the gloom, no matter the cost,
Life persists, though dreams are tossed.

Shadows dance beneath the pines,
Echoes soft in twisted lines.
Frozen tales that fate defines,
Every heartbeat intertwines.

In the quiet, a spark ignites,
Casting shadows, drawing sights.
In the depths of winter's nights,
Hope emerges, love ignites.

Beneath the surface, life runs deep,
As icy winds begin to sweep.
In the secrets that we keep,
Winter sings while others sleep.

Elysium of the Frozen Woods

In a realm where silence reigns,
Frosted branches, nature's chains.
Beauty captured, no restraints,
In this land where love remains.

Gentle whispers in the trees,
Carried softly by the breeze.
In the stillness, we find ease,
Amidst the frost, our hearts please.

Each snowflake tells a story,
Of fleeting joys, of fleeting glory.
In this woods of pure allegory,
Dreams unravel, a quiet quarry.

Through the mist and icy air,
Traces left that once were there.
In the frozen world, we share,
Moments woven with utmost care.

Elysium where spirits soar,
In the chill, we beg for more.
Underneath the winter's core,
Love will thrive forevermore.

Echoes of Winter's Heart

In the break of dawn so pale,
Winter breathes in softest wail.
Echoes linger in the gale,
Nature whispers, old as tale.

Every flake, a tale they tell,
Of frosty nights that cast a spell.
In this realm, we dwell so well,
In the stillness, hearts rebel.

Crackling fires give warmth and light,
Against the cold, we hold on tight.
Echoes echo in the night,
In winter's arms, all feels right.

Memories dance and weave around,
In the quiet, love is found.
With every stir, every sound,
Echoes of winter's heart abound.

Together wrapped in snowy dreams,
Life like a flowing stream redeems.
In this season, hope redeems,
Eternal bonds, like moonbeams.

Glimmering Crystals at Dawn

Morning light spills gold,
Over hills and open fields,
Crystals glimmer in the dew,
Nature's jewels softly revealed.

A breath of calm surrounds,
Awakening the sleepy trees,
Whispers in the gentle breeze,
Singing softly, nature's sounds.

Birds take flight with grace,
Leaving trails in the azure sky,
While shadows dance and play,
As the sun begins to rise.

Each ray a soft embrace,
Kissing petals, bright and warm,
The world begins to wake,
Cocooned in a golden charm.

In the quiet of the morn,
Promises of new beginnings,
Hope sparkles in the air,
A brand new day is spinning.

Icy Veins of a Sleepy Wood

Beneath the shivering leaves,
A whisper of the winter chill,
Branches arch like ancient bones,
Time stands still, the world is still.

Footsteps crunch on brittle frost,
Every sound, a crystal clear,
Echoes through the silent boughs,
Nature's breath, so close yet dear.

Shadows flicker in the light,
As sunbeams pierce the icy veil,
Patterns weave upon the ground,
Stories told in silver trail.

In this realm of frozen dreams,
Magic flows through every vein,
A symphony of frost and calm,
Awakens beauty long contained.

Here, time weaves a tapestry,
Of slumber deep, of dreams untold,
In icy veins of sleepy woods,
The heart of winter, brave and bold.

Beneath the Snowy Canopy

Softly draped in winter's quilt,
The world is blanketed in white,
Beneath the snowy canopy,
Lies a world of pure delight.

Branches bow with a heavy crown,
As snowflakes dance in the cool air,
Every flake a whispered secret,
Nature's breath, tender and rare.

A hush falls over everything,
As footprints trace the hidden path,
Wonders waiting to be seen,
In the quiet aftermath.

Icicles hang like chandeliers,
Glistening in the pale moonlight,
Each glimmer holds a story dear,
Of winter's beauty, pure and bright.

Within this peaceful, frozen realm,
Hearts are still and spirits high,
Beneath the snowy canopy,
The world breathes softly, a gentle sigh.

Ethereal Trails of Ice and Time

Ghostly forms of ice arise,
In the stillness of the night,
Trails of beauty, sharp and clear,
As moonlight bathes the world in light.

Footprints of a fleeting past,
Imprints etched on frozen ground,
Each one tells a tale of dreams,
Whispers lost, so rarely found.

Frosted glass on every pane,
Captures moments, quick and frail,
Ephemeral as a breath's wisp,
In the dance of time, we sail.

Ethereal paths wind and weave,
Through the silvered, sonorous night,
Each step a soft remembrance,
Of the beauty held in twilight.

So we wander through the frost,
Guided by the stars above,
In trails of ice, we seek the truth,
In every breath, we find our love.

Adventures on Shimmering Trails

Beneath the stars, we roam the night,
With laughter soft, in moon's soft light.
Each step a story, each glance a thrill,
On shimmering trails, our hearts do fill.

Through whispering woods, and rivers bright,
We chase the dawn, break free from plight.
With open hearts and skies so wide,
Together we venture, side by side.

The world awakes with colors bold,
In every moment, new dreams unfold.
With nature's magic, we forge our way,
On shimmering trails, forever we stay.

The echoes of laughter, the scent of pine,
In this adventure, your hand in mine.
With every sunset, our spirits soar,
On shimmering trails, we yearn for more.

Together, we'll dance on the edge of time,
In the warmth of friendship, the rhythm of rhyme.
Each day a canvas, each night a song,
On shimmering trails, where we belong.

Secrets Beneath the Frozen Surface

Ice-bound whispers, where silence reigns,
Beneath the surface, hidden pains.
A world encased in crystal sheen,
Secrets lie where few have been.

Glistening shadows dance in the cold,
Stories untold, they silently hold.
As winter breathes, the cosmos sighs,
In frozen depths, the past still lies.

The moonlight glimmers on sheets of glass,
Reflecting dreams of seasons past.
Beneath the ice, hope flickers bright,
Yearning for warmth, for the return of light.

Yet in the freeze, there's beauty found,
A tranquil peace, a soft surround.
With every layer, a tale unfolds,
In secrets deep, the heart beholds.

So heed the whispers, feel the call,
Of secrets woven in nature's thrall.
Beneath the frozen surface, we find
The timeless stories, entwined and blind.

The Cold Embrace of Twilight

As evening falls, the sky bleeds blue,
In twilight's arms, the world feels new.
With shadows dancing, the stars take flight,
In the cold embrace of coming night.

Crimson edges blend with gray,
The sun retreats, it's time to play.
A hush wraps round, a gentle sigh,
As day surrenders to the sky.

The air grows crisp, the whispers low,
In twilight's hold, the spirits flow.
With every breath, a canvas drawn,
In twilight's grasp, we find the dawn.

Flickers of light, the fireflies gleam,
In shadows cast, we weave a dream.
Together we stand, our hearts in tune,
Under the watch of the silver moon.

In the stillness, magic brews,
In the cold embrace, we find our clues.
For in the twilight, love shines bright,
In the soft glow of the approaching night.

Frost-kissed Memories Awaken

In the morning light, the frost does gleam,
Awakening whispers of a distant dream.
Each crystal formed tells a silent tale,
Of laughter and love, where memories prevail.

With every breath, the air feels pure,
Frost-kissed moments, we must endure.
In chilly embraces, the past revives,
In the warmth of memories, our spirit thrives.

Through fields of white, we wander free,
Where echoes linger, where we used to be.
Each step a dance on this glistening ground,
In frost-kissed memories, joy is found.

The sun breaks through, melting the ice,
Revealing stories, a hidden paradise.
With every glance, history awakens,
In frost-kissed hues, our heart's unshaken.

So cherish the moments, hold them tight,
In the embrace of the frosty light.
For every memory, sweet and plain,
In frost-kissed dreams, love will remain.

Enchanted Steps on White Powder

In a world where silence reigns,
Footsteps carve the snow like dreams,
Each step a story softly told,
Whispers of magic in the cold.

Twinkling stars adorn the night,
Reflecting paths of purest white,
A journey wrapped in crystal glow,
Where time stands still, and spirits flow.

Beneath the trees, the shadows dance,
In frosted wonder, they entrance,
A glimpse of beauty, rare and bright,
In winter's hold, a heart takes flight.

The moonlight casts its silver beams,
Upon the drifts, where hope redeems,
And as I wander through the frost,
I find the pieces I thought lost.

With every breath, the cold embrace,
Wraps around me, like a lace,
These enchanted steps, they lead me home,
In endless winter, I will roam.

Frosty Whispers in Lonesome Glades

In lonesome glades, the whispers sigh,
Frosty breath from trees up high,
Crystals glimmer, secrets to share,
Underneath the evening air.

Footsteps crunch on frozen ground,
In solitude, my heart is found,
Echoes of laughter, long since gone,
In shadows cast by the fading dawn.

Nature's voice, a gentle call,
Through branches bare, I hear it all,
Whispers soft as winter's breath,
Remind me of the warmth in death.

Beneath the veil of frost and haze,
Time stretches thin in quiet ways,
Each frozen tear a memory bright,
In lonesome glades, I seek the light.

As twilight sinks, the skies turn gray,
In frost's embrace, I find my way,
Amongst the whispers, still I stand,
Connected to this lonesome land.

Veil of Ice and Solitude

A veil of ice drapes o'er the scene,
In solitude, the world feels keen,
The crispness bites, yet beauty stays,
In frozen frames of winter's gaze.

In quiet corners, shadows blend,
With frosty patterns, shapes extend,
Each breath a cloud, a moment's pause,
In nature's grasp, I find my cause.

Silence deep, a sacred ground,
Where echoes of the heart resound,
Among the pines and fallen leaves,
The chill embraces, softly weaves.

A tapestry of white and gray,
Where solitude invites to play,
Amidst the stillness, strength is found,
In every flake that graces ground.

So here I stand, where moments freeze,
In a veil of ice, my spirit flees,
To touch the whispers of the night,
In solitude, I find my light.

Pathways Beneath Winter's Gaze

Beneath the frost, the pathways lie,
Each step a path beneath the sky,
In winter's gaze, I roam and drift,
Amidst the chill, the heart can lift.

Gentle flakes fall, a silent grace,
Covering all in a soft embrace,
Footprints left in the freshly laid,
In winter's spell, dreams won't fade.

Whispers linger as shadows play,
In this wonderland, I find my way,
The world transformed, a canvas white,
Beneath the stars, I take flight.

Voices carried on the breeze,
In tangled branches, secrets tease,
With every breath, the cold bites deep,
Yet in this magic, dreams I keep.

So onward bound, I greet the night,
With every step, a spark ignites,
In winter's heart, I feel alive,
On pathways where the dreams arrive.

Beneath a Blanket of Sparkling Silence

In the hush of winter's breath,
Stars twinkle like distant gems.
Snowflakes dance in silent grace,
Wrapped in a soft, icy hem.

Moonlight paints the world in white,
Whispers carry through the trees.
A quilt of calm holds tight,
Cradled in the night's gentle freeze.

Each footstep leaves a fleeting mark,
In the stillness, echoes fade.
Nature's peace ignites a spark,
As dreams in frost begin to wade.

Underneath this tranquil sky,
Hearts find solace, hearts find cheer.
In icy stillness, we rely,
On warmth that blooms when love is near.

So let us linger in this scene,
Beneath a blanket soft and bright.
In sparkling silence, we are seen,
Connected in the beauty of night.

Journey of the Icebound Soul

Through frozen fields where shadows creep,
An icebound soul begins to roam.
With every step, the silence deep,
A quest for warmth, a search for home.

Mountains loom with ancient grace,
Crystals gleam like forgotten dreams.
In this vast, enchanted space,
Hope flickers through the frosty seams.

Oceans whisper to the air,
Echoes of tales long swept away.
Yet in the heart, a flame lays bare,
Guiding through the coldest day.

Through twilight's chill and dawn's embrace,
The journey winds, it's long and true.
Each breath I take, a quiet trace,
Of warmth that waits beyond the blue.

In the depths of glacial night,
A flicker glows, a compass found.
The icebound soul, fueled by light,
Moves forward, breaking icy ground.

Wandering Through Glacial Dreams

Wandering through the cold expanse,
Each breath a whisper in the air.
I find myself in nature's dance,
Lost in wonder, unaware.

Frozen rivers twist and glide,
Mirrored skies reflect my soul.
In these depths, I cannot hide,
As echoes pull me towards my goal.

Gentle winds weave tales of old,
Carrying stories from the past.
In glacial dreams, the heart is bold,
Searching for the shadows cast.

Footsteps mark the path I take,
In solitude, I find my way.
Each moment, like a crystal flake,
Shimmers bright, then fades to gray.

Through this realm of ice and night,
I wander lightly, free of chains.
Embracing both the dark and light,
In glacial dreams, my spirit gains.

Paths of Crystal and Shadow

Paths of crystal lead me near,
Where shadows linger in the cold.
A secret world, both bright and drear,
Where tales of silence dare be told.

Glistening light breaks through the dark,
Illuminating steps with care.
Each echo carries a soft spark,
A gentle touch, a whispered prayer.

Amidst these trails, both sharp and smooth,
Old souls wander, searching still.
In the frost, they find their groove,
Chasing dreams with iron will.

Here where shadows twist and sway,
The heart learns well to navigate.
In the cold, I trust the way,
And find my peace within fate.

With every step, I feel the call,
Of paths that intertwine and glide.
In crystal's grace, I rise and fall,
Forever lost, forever tied.

In the Grasp of the Silent Cold

Whispers drift on icy air,
A world hidden, dark and bare.
Trees stand silent, wear the frost,
Time feels timeless, beauty lost.

Moonlight dances on the snow,
Casting shadows, soft and slow.
Each breath a cloud, crisp and clear,
A moment seized, winter near.

Night wraps all in a silken shroud,
Nature sleeps, deep and proud.
Stars like diamonds fiercely glow,
In the grasp of the silent cold.

Footsteps crunch on powdered ground,
Echoes of a life profound.
Frigid breezes kiss the skin,
A chilling touch where warmth begins.

Time stands still through winter's beat,
In this maze, I find my feet.
Embraced by frost, I wander forth,
In the silent cold, I find my worth.

Veils of Winter's Ethereal Soul

Glistening snow, a gentle veil,
Whispers of winter's ghostly trail.
Beneath the cloak, life still remains,
Hidden dreams in frozen chains.

Silvery light on snowflakes twirls,
Dancing softly as the wind swirls.
Echoes of silence, a sweet refrain,
Veils of winter call my name.

I walk through realms of frosted grace,
Each step a tender, soft embrace.
Bare branches cradle fleeting skies,
Amidst the cold, the heart still flies.

Frozen rivers across the land,
Mirror moments, nature's hand.
In ethereal light, the world suspends,
As winter's soul softly blends.

In the hush, I find my peace,
Nature's artistry, a sweet release.
Veils of winter weave their glow,
Embracing all, both fast and slow.

Haunting Beauty in Glacial Landscapes

Mountains loom with ancient grace,
Carved by time in a cold embrace.
Rivers of ice, so slow they creep,
In their shadows, secrets sleep.

Frozen whispers echo wide,
In glacial depths where shadows hide.
Behold the beauty, stark yet bright,
In haunting stillness, day meets night.

Crystals sparkle where light meets dark,
Nature's canvas, a cold stark arc.
Breath of winter paints the scene,
A tapestry of white and green.

A castle made of ice and stone,
Whispers history, a voice alone.
Among the shards where silence reigns,
Beauty lives, despite the pains.

In glacial landscapes, I stand still,
Nature's heart, a gentle thrill.
Haunting beauty speaks so loud,
In whispers faint, I am enshrouded.

An Enchanted Journey Through Ice

Paths untrodden, caves of frost,
Adventure calls, no matter the cost.
Through the chill, I make my way,
Each heartbeat strong, night meets day.

Glistening walls, a dreamer's sight,
Illuminated by pale moonlight.
Icicles drip like tear-filled eyes,
In nature's grasp, my spirit flies.

Echoes of laughter, whispers of dreams,
Flow through the air like silver streams.
An enchanted journey, wild and free,
Where every moment is magic to me.

Frost-kissed air, a breath divine,
As time unwinds, stars intertwine.
Each step leads to a story unknown,
In the heart of winter, I find my home.

Paths of ice and shadows entwine,
Every turn brings a new design.
Through the silence, the journey unfolds,
An enchanted saga in winter holds.

Silent Crystals Beneath Moonlight

Beneath the cloak of midnight skies,
Silent crystals softly rise.
Glimmers dance on silver streams,
Whispers float like fragile dreams.

In the stillness, shadows play,
Moonlit paths where fairies sway.
Every sparkle, magic spun,
In the silence, two become one.

The world hushed under lunar light,
Nature sighs in pure delight.
Crystals shimmer, heartbeats blend,
In this moment, time can't end.

Branches bow with icy grace,
In their arms, the stars embrace.
Silent echoes, soft and sweet,
Where the earth and cosmos meet.

Every breath a sacred hymn,
In the night, the fears grow dim.
As the dawn begins to rise,
Morning steals the crystal skies.

Chilling Whispers of Winter's Breath

Whispers curl in the frosty air,
Chilling dreams without a care.
Snowflakes fall like feathered sighs,
While the world in silence lies.

Windows frost with icy lace,
Winter wraps the earth in grace.
Trees stand tall in quiet might,
Guardians of the chilly night.

Footsteps crunch in crisp white trails,
Tales of frost in whispered pales.
Each soft breath a cloud of steam,
Caught in the magic winter's dream.

Underneath the pale moon's glow,
Ghostly figures dance in snow.
Echoes of laughter fill the glades,
In this hush, the warmth cascades.

As the sun begins its fight,
Chilling whispers fade to light.
Winter bows to springtime's call,
Yet the memories linger, enthrall.

Echoes of a Frozen Journey

In the distance, echoes play,
Of a journey marked in gray.
Footprints linger on the frost,
In this world, what's gained, what's lost?

Frozen whispers through the trees,
Carried softly by the breeze.
Every breath a cloud of white,
Tracing paths by starry night.

Mountains stand in regal pride,
Guiding souls on winter's ride.
With each step the heartbeats thrum,
Through the snow, a rhythm hums.

Time is still, yet winds will sway,
Shadows dance in bright array.
Through the cold, the spirits soar,
Echoing tales from days of yore.

As the sun begins to rise,
Painting warmth across the skies,
Frozen echoes start to wane,
But the journey shall remain.

Shadows on the Icy Trail

Shadows stretch across the night,
On the trail, a ghostly light.
Footsteps crunch on brittle snow,
Where the icy breezes blow.

Every turn reveals a dream,
Silent rivers gently gleam.
In the stillness, whispers creep,
Secrets that the woods must keep.

Branches sway with icy breath,
Carrying tales of life and death.
Yet in darkness, hope ignites,
Guiding souls through winter's bites.

Around the bend, the moonlight glows,
Lighting paths where nobody goes.
Shadows dance beneath the trees,
Swaying gently in the breeze.

As dawn breaks with gentle fire,
Shadows fade and spirits tire.
But the trail, a timeless song,
Whispers of where hearts belong.

Steps imprinted in Glacial Dreams

In the hush of frosty night,
Footprints in snow, a silent flight.
Whispers of ice, a tale unfolds,
Within the shimmer, a dream that holds.

Glimmers of stars on a cold, clear sky,
Reflect on paths where moments lie.
Each step echoes, a gentle call,
Frozen dreams where the heart may stall.

Winds weave stories, soft and low,
In glacial realms where only few go.
Underneath the moon's tender gaze,
Dancing shadows in a cold haze.

Crystals of time, suspended bright,
Marking desires in pure white light.
With every breath, the chill descends,
Nature's promise that never ends.

In silence, beauty is found,
As glacial dreams wrap all around.
A canvas of winter, complete,
Where earth and sky are destined to meet.

Nature's Frozen Diary

Each flake a word in nature's pen,
Written softly, again and again.
Pages of ice stretched far and wide,
Chronicles kept where secrets abide.

Whispers of wind on a winter's path,
Guarding the tales of nature's wrath.
In frozen spaces, the stories grow,
Woven in frost, with a silvery glow.

Footsteps mark where the wild things roam,
In nature's diary, they find a home.
Nature declares her peace so true,
In each frozen line, a timeless view.

Sunrise breaks with a golden brush,
Highlighting moments in a hushed hush.
Quietly written in layers of snow,
Nature's voice in a gentle flow.

Beneath the stillness, a world unfolds,
Of winter's treasures, adventures bold.
In every shimmer, a tale is spun,
Nature's frozen diary, never done.

Voyage through Glacial Stillness

On the edge of silence, we drift and glide,
Through icy waters, where dreams reside.
The world is a canvas, painted so slow,
With shades of blue in the winter's glow.

A voyage beckons, through hush and grace,
In the realm where the wild thoughts race.
With every heartbeat, the frost does sigh,
In stillness found beneath the sky.

A serene journey, the heart takes flight,
Through mirrored realms where day meets night.
Crystal reflections, a sacred space,
Holding the echoes of nature's face.

Floating through dreams on a chilling breeze,
With whispers of stillness, my soul finds peace.
In the vast expanse, the spirit roams free,
On a glacial voyage, just nature and me.

Time slows down in the icy embrace,
Each moment captured, frame by frame.
In glacial stillness, we find our tune,
A dance of purity beneath the moon.

Frosted Memories in Still Air

In the cradle of winter, memories freeze,
Cascading whispers in the quiet trees.
Frosted dreams upon the ground,
Echoing moments where peace is found.

Woven in silence, the past awakes,
As shadows dance for the heart it takes.
Each breath a crystal, a story to tell,
In the icy realm where night dispels.

Hues of twilight, soft and bright,
Blanket the earth in gentle light.
Frosted memories linger near,
In the stillness, they reappear.

A fleeting touch of the winter's breath,
Carving the paths of life and death.
In each frosty exhale, echoes rise,
Residing deep in the frozen skies.

With every shimmer, a thought takes flight,
Frosted memories in the still night.
Time holds its breath, as dreams unfold,
In the arms of winter, tales retold.

The Enchanted Silence of Snow

In the night, a blanket white,
Softly covers all in sight.
Whispers dance on frosted air,
Stillness reigns everywhere.

Moonlight glimmers on each flake,
Magic stirs, begins to wake.
Each step taken, gentle hush,
Nature pauses in the rush.

Footprints left, a tale to tell,
In the silence, secrets dwell.
Stars peer down with twinkling eyes,
In the night, the magic lies.

Branches bow with snowy crowns,
Woven threads of winter gowns.
Underneath this frozen spell,
Peaceful hearts, they breathe so well.

Echoes fade, as dreams ignite,
In the calm of tranquil night.
The world pauses, breath abates,
In the snow, all hope awaits.

Glinting Frost Beneath Footfalls

Morning breaks with glinting light,
Frosty crystals, bold and bright.
Each step crunches, whispers low,
On the path where no one goes.

Sunrise paints the world in gold,
Stories of the brave and bold.
Nature sparkles, pure and clear,
In this moment, dreams draw near.

Breath comes out in clouds of white,
Footfalls dance, a fleeting sight.
Crisp air tingles on the skin,
In the chill, new dreams begin.

Glancing at the trees so bare,
Frosted branches, dreams laid bare.
Whispers echo through the dawn,
In this world, we carry on.

Every shadow tells a tale,
In the frost, we will not fail.
With each step, the day unfolds,
Glinting treasures yet untold.

Winter's Grasp on Forgotten Paths

In the woods, where few have tread,
Winter's grasp, a blanket spread.
Silent tales of those before,
Echo softly, folklore's lore.

Footprints lead to places lost,
In the depths, we count the cost.
Whispers linger, soft and shy,
Underneath the endless sky.

Branches hang, heavy with snow,
Where the gentle breezes blow.
Lost in time, the maps unwind,
Every turn, a path to find.

Frozen streams and icy trails,
Nature's gifts in winter gales.
A journey rich with spectral light,
Guided by the starry night.

In this realm, where spirits play,
Find your heart, let worries sway.
Winter's whisper, sweet and low,
Leads the way through fallen snow.

Frost-Kissed Whispers of the Trees

In the glade where shadows creep,
Frost-kissed branches softly weep.
Each twig whispers ancient lore,
Secrets hidden at their core.

Leaves long gone, yet spirits hum,
Winter's breath, a soothing drum.
Underneath the blanket white,
Life's embrace in chilly night.

Hushed confessions in the cold,
Nature's blankets, tales untold.
Every bough extends a hand,
Inviting dreams to understand.

Frosty lace upon the bark,
Guides us through the woods so dark.
In this silence, worlds unite,
Frosty whispers, pure delight.

As the moon fades into dawn,
Nature stirs, the night is gone.
In each breath, the magic gleams,
Frost-kissed paths lead into dreams.

The Glacial Heart Beats Softly

In silence deep, where stillness reigns,
A heartbeat echoes through icy chains.
Fragments of dreams in twilight's breath,
A soft pulse lingers, dancing with death.

Shadows embrace the glimmering light,
Shards of blue in the softest night.
Forgotten whispers of winter's grace,
Softly unfold in this frozen space.

Each flake a story, a memory spun,
Carried away by the warmth of the sun.
Yet here they rest, in crystallized art,
Where the glacial heart beats softly, apart.

Time loses meaning in this vast expanse,
Nature's own tune in a dreamlike dance.
The rhythm of cold and warmth intertwine,
A symphony played in the heart's design.

Deep in the silence, a truth does awaken,
The glacial heart, though seemingly shaken.
Holds in its core a warmth, so rare,
That life continues, hidden in the air.

Wandering Through Sparkling Shadows

In the twilight hour, shadows take flight,
Wandering softly, on edges of light.
Each step a secret, a story untold,
A dance through the darkness, with sparkles of gold.

Beneath the stars, the cosmos conspires,
To weave in the night, vibrant dreams of fires.
Echoing laughter, a ghostly refrain,
Through paths where the starlight and silence remain.

With every heartbeat, the shadows grow long,
A hymn of the night, a crystalline song.
Wandering onward, the sky starts to fade,
Into the whispers of twilight's cascade.

Sparkling wonders, the night softly gleams,
Materializing the fabric of dreams.
Footprints in starlight, a fleeting embrace,
Mark the journey through shadows with grace.

In the embrace of the dark, there's a spark,
A hint of the dawn, a promise so stark.
As light breaks anew, the shadows retreat,
Yet in our hearts, their magic is sweet.

The Dance of the Snowflakes

Delicate whispers fall from above,
Each flake a symbol, a gesture of love.
Twisting and twirling, a graceful ballet,
The dance of the snowflakes, in winter's display.

Glistening diamonds, spun from the air,
A tapestry woven with utmost care.
Drifting down softly, they gather and weave,
A blanket of wonder, the heart believes.

In the stillness of night, their elegance shines,
Swaying together in invisible lines.
A moment of magic, a fleeting chance,
To witness the beauty of winter's romance.

Every flake unique, a masterpiece bold,
Stories in silence, yet to be told.
They dance with the wind, a flicker of grace,
Embracing the earth in a soft, loving embrace.

As dawn breaks the spell, their journey is done,
Inherited rhythms of frost and the sun.
Yet the dance lives on in the heart of the day,
A memory lingers, in a snowflake's sway.

Underneath the Icebound Canopy

Beneath the frost, there lies a world bright,
A canopy woven of shimmering white.
In chill and in stillness, secrets abide,
Whispers of life in the silence reside.

The trees wear their coats of ethereal lace,
Holding the sparkle of winter's embrace.
Branches entwined in a frozen sigh,
Beneath the icebound canopy, dreams lie.

Footsteps muffled, the earth's breath is slow,
Each heartbeat a rumor in the soft glow.
The echoes of seasons drift far from the past,
Underneath the canopy, shadows are cast.

In the depths of the frost, life dances unseen,
In rhythms of nature, serene and keen.
A chorus of silence, a heartbeat of peace,
Underneath the icebound, where moments don't cease.

As morning awakens with a soft gentle hue,
The world stirs and stretches, embracing anew.
Yet shadows of winter linger and play,
Underneath the canopy, they softly sway.

Winter's Breath on Lonely Trails

Frosty whispers roam the night,
As shadows dance in silver light.
Footprints vanish, lost in snow,
The world sleeps soft beneath its glow.

Trees stand tall, their branches bare,
A quiet peace hangs in the air.
Each breath whispers tales anew,
Of winter's kiss, pure, sweet, and true.

In the stillness, hearts align,
With nature's rhythm, divine design.
Moonlight bathes the paths we tread,
Where dreams awaken, softly spread.

The world seems small, the night, so vast,
As memory drifts, fading past.
With every step, the silence calls,
In winter's breath, the spirit sprawls.

Through lonely trails, cold winds will sweep,
Leaving traces for time to keep.
In the depths of night, we find our way,
A journey bound in winter's sway.

The Crystal Silence of Night

In the hush, the stars take flight,
A silver crown adorns the night.
Whispers float on chilly air,
In a world of crystal, rare and fair.

Moonbeams dance on frozen streams,
Casting shadows, weaving dreams.
Each twinkle speaks of promises,
In silence wrapped, nature's caress.

Snowflakes fall like fleeting sighs,
Painting earth with white disguise.
The night unfolds its gentle arms,
Embracing all with subtle charms.

Through the dark, a soft glow shines,
Guiding hearts along the lines.
In the crystal silence, we shall find,
The peace that dwells within the mind.

A symphony of quiet bliss,
In every breath, a tender kiss.
As night whispers, dreams take flight,
In the crystal silence of the night.

Midnight's Dance on Frozen Ground

At the stroke of midnight's chime,
Moonlit shadows twist and climb.
The frosty earth, a glimmering stage,
Where winter's dancers break the cage.

With every step, the silence sways,
In harmony with nature's plays.
The whispers of the wind invite,
A ballet born of purest light.

Sculpted shapes, the snowflakes twirl,
In a world where magic unfurls.
The stars become our guiding fire,
As night unveils its wild desire.

Chilled air wraps around us tight,
In this embrace, we feel the light.
The frozen ground beneath our feet,
Cradles dreams, oh so sweet.

As midnight dances, spirits soar,
In the beauty that we can't ignore.
With every heartbeat, time stands still,
On frozen ground, we find our will.

Path of the Winter Solstice

On winter's edge, the solstice glows,
With golden light, the season knows.
A path unfolds beneath the trees,
In whispered winds, a gentle breeze.

Days grow short, but dreams stay bright,
Illuminated by the stars' soft light.
Each step we take, the earth in trance,
Guides us on through winter's dance.

Crystal branches, etched in frost,
Holding memories, never lost.
In the stillness, hopes arise,
As nature weaves its lullabies.

Through shadows deep and valleys wide,
We walk with courage, hearts open wide.
In the chill, a promise stirs,
Of warmth that whispers, love endures.

So guide us forth, oh winter's glow,
On paths where only dreamers go.
The solstice sings, the night entwined,
In the sacred silence, we unbind.

The Stillness of a Crystal Dawn

In the hush of morning light,
A crystal dawn begins to rise,
Shimmering on the frosty ground,
Nature's breath, a soft disguise.

Whispers float in silent air,
As shadows dance on silver trees,
Each moment holds a quiet prayer,
A world at peace, a gentle peace.

The sun peeks through with golden rays,
Painting skies in shades of pink,
In this stillness, the heart sways,
Inviting all to pause and think.

The frosted leaves, a jeweled sheen,
Every branch a sparkling dream,
In the stillness, there's a scene,
A canvas touched by nature's theme.

As daylight breaks, the shadows flee,
Yet the calm forever lingers,
In this moment, we are free,
Bound by the magic in our fingers.

Icebound Echoes of Solitude

In an expanse of glistening white,
Where quiet whispers reign supreme,
Icebound echoes take their flight,
A frozen world, a waking dream.

Footsteps crunch on snow-kissed ground,
Each breath a mist upon the air,
Solitude in silence found,
Nature's beauty, stark and rare.

The trees wear coats of shimmering frost,
While shadows play in twilight's glow,
In isolation, none are lost,
In soft embraces, hearts will grow.

Still waters hold the midnight stars,
Reflecting truths we rarely see,
In icebound realms, we've come so far,
Discovering who we long to be.

The world beyond in chaos swirls,
But here, the mind finds gentle space,
In icy depths, the heart unfurls,
And solitude becomes our grace.

Frost-Laden Breezes of Reflection

Beneath the veil of frosted air,
The trees stand tall, a silent crew,
A whispering breeze calls us there,
To reflect on the world we knew.

With every breath, the crispness sings,
Nature's voice in whispers clear,
Frost-laden winds such truth brings,
Stirring memories, drawing near.

Each flake that falls a tale retold,
Of seasons past, of love and loss,
In the chill, our dreams unfold,
In quiet moments, bear the cross.

As winter wraps its arms around,
We gather warmth from within our souls,
In reflection, newfound ground,
A fire burning, making us whole.

In frost's embrace, we find the light,
Illuminating paths once lost,
Through breezes crisp, our spirits bright,
As we reflect, no matter the cost.

Dreaming Under a Crown of Frost

Beneath the stars, the night is still,
A crown of frost on slumbering trees,
Dreams take flight, as thoughts distill,
In this realm, the heart's at ease.

The moonlight dances on frozen ground,
Casting shadows, silver and rare,
In the silence, magic's found,
Underneath its gleaming glare.

Each breath of night, a lullaby,
Wrapped in warmth of icy air,
Echoes of wishes drift and sigh,
Dreams entwined in the cool night's care.

A crown of frost adorns the earth,
With every sparkle, a wish made true,
In dreams, we find new sense of worth,
As morning whispers, the sky turns blue.

While the world wakes with dawning light,
We carry remnants of the night,
In dreams, we dared to soar so high,
Beneath the frost, our spirits fly.

Icy Murmurs of a Hidden World

In the silence of the glade,
Whispers of frost softly played.
Branches bow with crystal tears,
Nature cloaked in frosty years.

Beneath the surface, life unfolds,
Stories waiting to be told.
Shadows dance with fleeting light,
In the heart of winter's night.

Frozen echoes fill the air,
Secrets hidden, soft and rare.
Each breath becomes a story spun,
In the glimmer of the sun.

Winds carry tales from afar,
Hushed dreams weave like a star.
Frost-kissed laughter, soft and mild,
In the heart of nature's child.

So listen close, let silence reign,
In this world, there's beauty gained.
Icy murmurs, soft and clear,
Speak of wonders, always near.

Dreaming in Frost and Time

In the stillness, dreams take flight,
Under blankets of silver light.
Frosted windows, a world aglow,
Time stands still beneath the snow.

Whispers float on chilly air,
Every moment, rich and rare.
Snowflakes dance like memories,
Carried on the winter's breeze.

Lost in visions of frozen grace,
Winter's touch leaves a gentle trace.
Each icicle, a crystal dream,
Flowing with a soft, bright gleam.

The moon dips low, a silver crest,
In this wonder, hearts find rest.
Memories wrapped in cold embrace,
Dreaming slowly, finding space.

As the night deepens its hold,
Stories of frost will be told.
In this moment, still and divine,
We are dreaming in frost and time.

A Journey Beneath the Frozen Stars

Stars awaken with a spark,
Guiding shadows through the dark.
Beneath the frost, the earth sleeps tight,
Journey whispers in the night.

Crisp and clear, the air does sing,
Hope awakens with the spring.
Each step taken, a tale unfolds,
Beneath the blanket of the cold.

Footprints marking where we roam,
In this night, we find our home.
Every heartbeat, every sigh,
Dances with the northern sky.

Silver rivers, icy flows,
Reflecting where the cold wind blows.
Stories etched in stars above,
A soft reminder, filled with love.

So onward still, with hearts so bold,
Under glimmers, red and gold.
A journey true beneath the light,
To find our way through frozen night.

Echoes of the Snowbound Night

Softly falling, flakes so bright,
Echoes dream of winter's night.
Silhouettes in the moon's embrace,
Time dissolving, leaves no trace.

Wind's caress on rooftops low,
Whispers stories wrapped in snow.
Candles flicker, warm and kind,
In their glow, peace we find.

Footsteps wandering, soft and slow,
Tracing paths where cold winds blow.
Silent woods, a canvas wide,
Holding secrets, deep inside.

With every breath, the chill runs deep,
In this night, our dreams now keep.
Softly, softly, the stars align,
In echoes of the snowbound time.

Let the world in slumber fall,
To nature's heart, we heed the call.
In this winter, calm and bright,
We embrace the snowbound night.

Ghosts of the Hallowed Frost

Whispers drift through the silent trees,
Veils of frost cling to the midnight breeze.
Shadows dance where the old heart lies,
Memories whisper under snowy skies.

Faint echoes of laughter lost to time,
Chiming softly like a distant chime.
In the chill, the past still breathes,
As the spirit of winter softly weaves.

Footprints linger on the icy ground,
Stories wrapped in the silence profound.
Each flake a tale, each breath a sigh,
Ghosts of the hallowed frost drift by.

From the shadows, eyes gleam with light,
Bound by frost, they dance in the night.
Echoes of joy knit the bitter air,
Life, death, and dreams mingle in despair.

Frozen laughter, a haunting sound,
Woven in the silence, softly profound.
The ghosts of winter can still ignite,
Hearts finding warmth in the hallowed night.

Lament of the Frozen Stream

Once it flowed with a joyous song,
Now it pools where the shadows throng.
Beneath the ice, a dream lies still,
Whispering secrets, haunted by will.

Branches weep over the frozen bed,
In their silence, the past is shed.
Faint echoes of the summer's gleam,
Haunt the edges of the frozen stream.

Raindrops freeze as they find repose,
Covering sorrow in soft, white glows.
Each ripple, a Remembrance shrouded tight,
Yearning for warmth, lost in the night.

Memories float like leaves in air,
Caught in twilight, tangled in despair.
Time stands still where the waters weep,
In this lament, the echoes seep.

The world forgets what the stream once knew,
As the currents whisper, soft and blue.
Frozen silence, a haunting seam,
Wrapped in the tale of the frozen stream.

Echoing Footfalls in the Chill Night

In the dark, only echoes remain,
Footfalls whispering through the pain.
Each step a tale of the winter harsh,
Carving paths in the moonlight's marsh.

Branches creak in the stillness tight,
Holding secrets in the chill night.
Voices of shadows lose their way,
Carried away on the winds of gray.

Footprints traced in the layer of white,
Guide the traveler through the long night.
Haunting melodies fill the air,
Woven within the chilling flare.

A shiver runs as the cold winds blow,
Ghostly figures in the soft glow.
Echoing laughter from places past,
Flickers and fades, but never lasts.

In the silence, stories unfold,
Carried in whispers, brave and bold.
As footfalls echo in the curve of time,
The chill night embraces, sweet and sublime.

The Glimpse of an Icy Horizon

Over the hills, the dawn unfolds,
Painting ice in hues of gold.
A silent glow, a world anew,
Within the frost, dreams break through.

Shimmering edges where earth meets sky,
Whispers of light, a soft goodbye.
The icy horizon, a beckoning call,
Nature's canvas, enchanting all.

A chill breathes through the valley's breath,
Life and sorrow entwined in death.
Fractured hopes beneath the sheen,
Each moment carved in shades of green.

Glistening wonders that time bestows,
Reflect the tales that winter knows.
A fleeting glimpse of what lies ahead,
In the icy horizon, dreams are fed.

Sunrise glows on the frozen land,
Painting stories with a gentle hand.
In the distance, visions ignite,
The icy horizon birthed in light.

Shimmering Silence of Hoarfrost

In the stillness, frost does weave,
Whispers of winter, soft as a leave.
A blanket of ice, a glimmering sheet,
Nature's quiet song, tender and sweet.

Branches adorned with crystal light,
Glistening jewels, tucked in the night.
Each breath hangs heavy, a frosty sigh,
Under the moon, where shadows lie.

Pine trees stand tall, draped in white,
Guardians of silence, cloaked from sight.
Footfalls echo on the frozen ground,
In shimmering silence, peace is found.

The world transformed, magic unfolds,
A tapestry spun with stories untold.
In the heart of winter, dreams take flight,
Embracing the calm, a gentle delight.

Moments linger, frozen in time,
In the silence, a whispered rhyme.
Hoarfrost dances, a delicate grace,
In the shimmering hush, nature's embrace.

Footprints on a Shimmering Scape

A canvas of white, so vast and bright,
Footprints appear, a curious sight.
Each step a story, sparked in the snow,
Mapping the journey where wanderers go.

The shimmer of frost underfoot gleams,
Dreams interwoven in winter's dreams.
Traces of laughter, new paths to chart,
In a shimmering scape, the world is art.

Crystal flashes where shadows collide,
With hope in the air, and warmth inside.
Nature's soft laughter, a guiding embrace,
Revealing the beauty of each sacred space.

Each heartbeat echoes through frozen air,
In the stillness of winter, we shed every care.
With every footprint, a tale unfolds,
In the shimmering depths, life's wisdom holds.

So wander with purpose, through the cold light,
Follow the whispers that beckon the night.
In the dance of the frost, let your spirit soar,
On this shimmering scape, forever explore.

Pathways Laced in Ice

Paths glisten bright, a crystalline maze,
Laced in the ice, where sunlight plays.
Each step taken, a caution to heed,
In the frozen beauty, adventure we need.

Frost-tipped branches cast long shadows,
Whispering secrets as gentle wind blows.
A world redefined in a coat of white,
Where dreams turn to stars on a clear winter night.

Winding and weaving through silence so deep,
With each icy breath, winter secrets we keep.
Guided by moonbeams and starlit skies,
In pathways laced, the spirit flies.

Every frozen moment, a tale to discern,
In the chill of the air, there's warmth to learn.
Navigating wonders, both calming and wild,
In the heartbeat of winter, we remain a child.

So step into magic, embrace the unknown,
In pathways laced, beauty is sown.
With courage and wonder, embark on this quest,
In the ice-bound world, find your heart's rest.

Journey Through Winter's Veil

A tapestry woven of silver and blue,
Winter's veil whispers, soft and true.
Footprints untraveled, paths yet to see,
In the heart of the storm, we shape our spree.

Winds carry stories, ancient and bold,
Through valleys of white, their tales unfold.
Snowflakes like letters, drift from above,
In the journey of winter, we discover love.

Pine-scented breezes, fresh and alive,
In the chilly expanse, we learn to thrive.
Each flake a dance, each gust a song,
In the still of the season, we all belong.

Embrace the magic where silence prevails,
In the heart of the woods, through winter's veils.
With hope as our compass, and light as our guide,
In the journey through winter, let joy abide.

So wrap yourself warmly, let go of the day,
In winter's embrace, we find our way.
With each step we take, in the frosty air,
The journey is timeless, a moment to share.

Whispers of Winter's Breath

The frost-kissed air whispers low,
As leaves of old drift down in slow.
Nature's hush wraps the land tight,
Embraced by the calm of the night.

Moonbeams dance on fields of white,
Illuminating the silent flight.
Gentle breezes weave through the trees,
Carrying secrets on the freeze.

Footprints traced in the powdery glow,
Tell stories only the cold winds know.
A cloak of stillness, serene and bright,
Winter whispers in the fading light.

Soft as dreams in the dark of the hour,
Each breath of chill holds a waking power.
Silhouettes move in the ghostly shade,
While memories of warmth begin to fade.

In the still of night, hearts feel the pull,
As shadows whisper, ever so full.
A cycle of life in this frozen land,
Woven together, nature's grand hand.

Chilling Echoes Beneath

Beneath the icy veil lies a tale,
Where stillness reigns and echoes sail.
Each sound is hushed, wrapped in white,
As darkness swathes the world in night.

Crystals gleam under the moon's gaze,
Reflecting secrets of winter's maze.
Whispers ripple through the silent air,
Chilling echoes, tender and rare.

The crunch of snow beneath each tread,
Stirs the silence where few have fled.
Nature's heartbeat, slow and deep,
In the shadows where spirits creep.

Branches bow under the weight they bear,
Holding memories of a world laid bare.
With every breeze, a ghostly sigh,
As stars flicker in the frozen sky.

In this realm where frost monsters dwell,
Chilling echoes weave their spell.
A peaceful solitude, vast and wide,
In whispers of winter, secrets abide.

Traces in White Silence

In the still of dawn, a blanket lies,
Covering the earth under quiet skies.
Every footprint tells a tale,
Of nature's flight on the cold, stark trail.

Silhouettes dance in the morning mist,
Where icy breath and warmth coexist.
Traces of laughter hang in the air,
Caught in the moment, a world so rare.

Trees stand tall with arms held high,
Embracing whispers that float on by.
Children's joy in the snowflakes' fall,
Echoes of laughter, a timeless call.

Soft glows emerge where shadows meet,
In the expanse of this winter treat.
Each flake a muse, drifting with grace,
Leaving their mark in this frozen place.

In the hush of white silence, hearts will see,
A world reborn, wild and free.
As the sun melts away the night's embrace,
Traces linger long in winter's grace.

Glacial Shadows Dance

In twilight's grip, shadows start to sway,
Glacial forms in a shimmering ballet.
They glide and twirl over night's soft breath,
A silent waltz, a dance with death.

Cool winds stir the frosty air,
Nature's whispers, delicate and rare.
Every flicker, a story to tell,
Of ancient realms in their crystal shell.

The moon reflects on icy lakes,
Cascading light as the darkness shakes.
In whispers of night, the chill incites,
A past entwined in serene delights.

Frosted branches frame the dance,
A tapestry woven with nature's chance.
As shadows merge into the gloom,
Mysteries linger in winter's womb.

In the heart of winter, shadows reconcile,
Through glacial dances, time stretches a while.
As dawn breaks free into morning's trance,
Echoes of winter's graceful dance.

Whispers of the Silent Woods

In the woods where shadows creep,
Whispers rise, secrets keep.
Leaves rustle, stories told,
Nature's hush, a heart of gold.

Moonlight dances on the stream,
Stars above, a distant dream.
Branches sway with gentle grace,
In their arms, we find our place.

Winter's breath upon the trees,
Carrying tales on the breeze.
Footsteps soft on frost-kissed ground,
In this silence, peace is found.

Echoes of the night so pure,
In the dark, we feel secure.
Every whisper, every sigh,
A reminder that we fly.

Guided by the woodland's heart,
Woven threads of nature's art.
In the stillness, we unite,
Whispers of the woods ignite.

Hushed Souls Through Frozen Fields

In the fields where silence reigns,
Hushed souls wander, shedding chains.
Snowflakes fall like whispered dreams,
Blanketing earth, soft as streams.

Footprints trace the frosty ground,
In the stillness, peace is found.
Gentle sighs of winter's breath,
Through the fields, a dance with death.

Stars overhead, cold and bright,
Guiding lost souls through the night.
Every whisper, every sigh,
In the twilight, spirits fly.

Bare branches stretch, fingers thin,
Echoes of warmth rise within.
Through the frost, we seek the light,
Hushed souls find their way to flight.

In the vastness, heartbeats blend,
Frozen fields, where dreams transcend.
In their silence, stories thrive,
Hushed souls through frost, alive.

Frosted Eyes on Winter's Horizon

Frosted eyes peer through the cold,
Glimmers of warmth, stories told.
Winter's breath a chilling sigh,
Painting the world, white up high.

Horizon glows with dawn's embrace,
Nature's art, a tranquil grace.
Every flake, a world unique,
In their beauty, silence speaks.

Frigid air, a crisp delight,
Stars fade gently with the night.
Glistening frost on branches sway,
Kissing the dawn of a new day.

Frosted eyes hold dreams of spring,
In the heart, a whispering.
Through the cold, we learn to wait,
Winter's song, a gentle fate.

With each breath, a promise flows,
In the stillness, hope still grows.
Frosted eyes on horizons wide,
Holding warmth that will abide.

Beyond the Icicle Veil

Beyond the veil of icy dreams,
Whispers echo, soft moonbeams.
Crystalline hung in twilight's grace,
Time moves slow in this sacred space.

Icicles drip, a melody,
Singing softly, wild and free.
In the shadows, secrets twine,
Stories linger, hearts align.

Winter's chill wraps all in white,
Guiding us through the cold night.
In the hush, we hear a call,
Beyond the veil, we'll never fall.

Snowflakes drift, a gentle sigh,
Painting the world, lullaby.
With every breath, dreams emerge,
Beyond the veil, feel the surge.

Hold on tight to fleeting light,
In the darkness, sparks ignite.
Beyond the icicle's embrace,
Lies the warmth of love's grace.

Milton Keynes UK
Ingram Content Group UK Ltd.
UKHW010229111224
452348UK00011B/625

9 789908 520995